CIRCLE BACK!

CIRCLE BACK!

The Little Book of
Business Buzzwords

George Baggaley

LONDON PUBLISHING PARTNERSHIP

Copyright © 2025 by George Baggaley

Published by London Publishing Partnership
www.londonpublishingpartnership.co.uk

All rights reserved. No part of this publication may be
reproduced, distributed, **elevated**, **shipped** or **pinged**
in any form without the prior written permission of
the author and publisher – except in the case of brief
quotations, or **nuggets**, in reviews and other
non-commercial purposes permitted by copyright law

ISBN: 978-1-916749-33-7 (hbk)
ISBN: 978-1-916749-34-4 (iPDF)
ISBN: 978-1-916749-35-1 (ePUB)

A catalogue record for this book is available
from the British Library

This book has been composed in Adobe Garamond Pro

Copy-edited and typeset by T&T Productions Ltd, London
www.tandtproductions.com

To collaborate, please **touch base** with the author via
circle.back@hotmail.com

The cartoons on pages v, 37 and 106 were
provided by the illustrator Mark Cowie (@tonyhantz)

The book can be ordered from the publisher's website
via the QR code below or from any other bookseller

Preface

The fourth edition of *Webster's New World College Dictionary* includes the following definitions.

Buzzword (noun): a word or phrase that has little or imprecise meaning but sounds impressive to outsiders.

Jargon (noun): the specialised vocabulary and idioms of those in the same work, profession, etc.

Taking the definitions above as a reference point, this book treats as a 'business buzzword' any term, metaphor, figure of speech or acronym that is used predominantly for work ('corporate') purposes. Business buzzwords differ from 'slang' in this regard, as slang includes words used elsewhere in our daily lives.

As a result, we omit common phrases such as 'hit it out the park' or 'that's an open goal'. It should be noted that the world of sport rivals that of business for being one of the great generators of buzzwords, with the military being another key area: some commentators believe that the origin of corporate jargon was returning World

War II soldiers bringing their military terminology into the workplace.*

Also ignored are technical phrases (and their acronyms) that exist due to an absence of credible or easy alternatives (e.g. AGM, for annual general meeting) as well as terms that are too company specific (such as MMH, which is used by Meta employees in place of 'make Mark [Zuckerberg] happy').

Instead, our focus is purely on office jargon that is deployed in place of perfectly good, old-fashioned, normal words. This is where the real *confusion* and *amusement* lie – emotions your author has kept in mind as guiding **north stars**.

In this regard, the book's objectives are twofold.

- To provide a legitimate dictionary for people to consult if they're stumped by their manager telling them to do things like **run an idea up the flagpole.**

- To poke a little fun at the pure abundance of business buzzwords as well as those who keep these words in circulation.

Which, ultimately, is all of us. Like most cultural phenomena, the captivating thing about the world of

---

* Lillian Stone. 2024. The animal instinct that drives workers to adopt corporate jargon. *BBC Worklife*, 5 February (https://www.bbc.com/worklife/article/20240202-the-animal-instinct-that-drives-workers-to-adopt-corporate-jargon).

corporate jargon is that it only exists through our own collective will and participation.

To help achieve the objectives above, example dialogue has been added beneath some definitions to help show the use of jargon in context. A cast of fictional characters (see the list in the next section) has been deployed to have these made-up conversations – almost all of which bear significant resemblance to the people and exchanges your author has come across while navigating his own path through the jargon minefield that is the modern world of work.

Our cast of characters

The example dialogue you will find in many of the buzzword definitions usually involves the staff of either Peddle PR or Slug Energy Ltd. Let me introduce to you to them.

Peddle PR – a public relations agency team

Sally Bright, intern
Smart, full of good ideas, far more capable than most of her superiors.

Jimmy Everyman, account executive
Trying and failing to climb the corporate ladder. Overworked and under-appreciated by management.

Chad Hubris, account manager
Rubbish at his job but looks and sounds the part. Gets by on bravado (being well versed in business buzzwords) and by getting his smarter subordinates (Sally and Jimmy) to do the work.

Elizabeth Shirks, account director
Sees day-to-day tasks as being beneath her now she is fairly senior. Line manager to a flock of tiresome account executives (including Jimmy) who she has little time for. Has perfected the art of appearing busy without doing a whole lot. Mentor to Chad.

Slug Energy Ltd – an in-house marketing team

Yasmin Newt, marketing intern
Bewildered by both the business world and the people that rule it. Starting to wonder if her marketing degree from Leeds Beckett University was worth the £50,000 of debt she accrued obtaining it.

Will Worksmore, marketing specialist
Slaving all hours beneath his jargon-connoisseur of a boss, Harriet. Rarely feels very special.

Harriet Stern (she/her/hers), head of marketing
Boss of Will. Ensures that her real personality (if it exists) is never exposed in the workplace. Likes her staff to attend the office five days a week – even if she does not.

Why do business buzzwords even exist? A short essay

A group of lads meet up in the pub.

Lad A: Who chose this pub again? I've never liked it.

Lad B: Well, if you'd bothered touching base in our WhatsApp thought shower, you could have suggested somewhere else. I even pinged you about it!

Lad A: It really needs up-levelling.

Lad C: Agreed. I'd start by elevating the toilets.

Lad A: Seen the Red Lion since its refurb? That's the hero establishment round here these days.

Lad B: Whatever – we're here now. Has everyone completed the actions in the workback plan I socialised?

Lad C: Yep, I onboarded Darren.

Darren: Cheers mate. Can't bloody wait for this!

Lad B: Glad you can make it this year. We're going full white glove. And the accommodation?

Lad A: Sorry lads, I haven't booked it yet.

Lad B:	FFS mate! We're flying to Ibiza four weeks today – this is mission critical!!
Lad A:	I've just been so snowed under.
Lad B:	Then delegate your deliverables! We can't miss any KPIs here.
Lad C:	I've got bandwidth.
Lad B:	OK, great. Can you get it done by EOP?

*

In a house across the street a husband and wife are talking.

Wife:	Let's get our ducks in a row regarding the Thompsons' garden party. We need to make a real thunder and lightning contribution …
Husband:	Tracking. Why don't I pick up a few bottles of wine from Tesco? I saw some Prosecco on discount the other day …
Wife:	Put a pin in that. Have you forgotten the Thompsons are wine thought leaders?! She's pretty much a Champagne evangelist these days. Tesco won't cut it.
Husband:	Hmm, we could always sync with Liam and Daisy and get an integrated gift?
Wife:	No, those two are on the bleeding edge. They'd have sorted this weeks ago and it'll be a real moonshot idea.

Husband:	The problem with the Thompsons is they've got everything. It's so hard to identify the whitespace!
Wife:	Let's circle back after we've put the kids to bed. When are we telling them they're migrating schools?
Husband:	I was going to open the kimono tomorrow …

*

Neither of these conversations has ever happened – at least with regard to the language used. Yet in the professional realm, such jargon-filled exchanges are commonplace.

So widely deployed are many of the terms featured above that we rarely stop to consider just how bizarre it is to reserve a separate vocabulary entirely for work purposes.

The rise of remote working has made this even weirder. Before, corporate jargon would only spew forth in a specific physical place: the office. But now, sitting with a laptop at the kitchen table, we're quite happy to switch from 'Can we have a quick huddle about the end-of-week roadmap?' to 'What's the plan this weekend?" depending on whether we're Zooming with a co-worker or chatting to a housemate who's just walked in to put the kettle on.

While the odd phrase becomes so well used it ceases to be seen as a buzzword at all, it's remarkable how few terms truly make the jump into common parlance.

But why is this? What makes us, en masse, reach for an alternative lexicon among colleagues? What makes those words thrive in the workplace but not outside of it? And why are some professions more prone to jargon than others?

A 2023 survey by LinkedIn and Duolingo, which interviewed thousands of people across eight countries, found that 58% of workers feel jargon is overused. Almost half (46%) wished jargon would go away altogether; 57% said that misunderstanding jargon wastes time; while 40% had made a mistake because they didn't know the meaning of a buzzword.

It's clearly not love or admiration that has fuelled jargon's rise, then. Part of the answer seems to lie in the search for *authority*.

'We use jargon when we're feeling insecure, to help us feel like we have a higher status,' says Professor Adam Galinsky (a professor of leadership and ethics at Columbia Business School) in a recent study about how we communicate at work.[*] Elsewhere, Zachariah Brown (a co-author of Galinsky's) attributes the use of jargon to a form of 'human peacocking'.[**]

---

[*] Zachariah C. Brown, Eric M. Anicich and Adam D. Galinsky. 2020. Compensatory conspicuous communication: low status increases jargon use. *Organizational Behavior and Human Decision Processes* **161**, 274–290 (https://www.sciencedirect.com/science/article/abs/pii/S0749597820303666).
[**] Lito Howse interview with Zach Brown. 2020. Feeling inferior? You're more likely to use jargon, study says. CBC Radio, 23 November (https://www.cbc.ca/radio/asithappens/as-it-happens-friday-edition-1.5809805/feeling-inferior-you-re-more-likely-to-use-jargon-study-says-1.5810338).

Desire for a sense of *belonging* is, perhaps, a more satisfactory theory. Not everyone craves *authority*, but feeling wanted or accepted is a deeper aspect of human nature that practically all of us are influenced by. The two, of course, are linked. Speaking the office lingo makes it more likely others will see us as credible, which, in turn, will make us feel more respected or more firmly embedded as part of the team. This has taken on additional importance for people who physically never see their colleagues and need to form strong bonds over the internet.

Both the notion of *worth* and its elusiveness are also major factors. *Worth* is at the heart of a famous study of modern work by the anthropology professor David Graeber, who published *Bullshit Jobs* in 2018. Graeber's book suggested that most modern occupations have no meaningful impact on society.

Between 1910 and 2000 the proportion of people in professional, managerial, sales and service jobs grew from one-quarter of total employment to three-quarters, observes Graeber. These modern – mostly white-collar – jobs, often spent largely staring at emails on a computer screen, can lack the sense of immediate achievement that comes more naturally with traditional forms of labour – ploughing a field, say, or building a wall or putting out a house fire. Given this lack of gratification, it makes sense for us to reach for terms that lend a sense of grandeur to roles that otherwise leave us feeling somewhat lacking in purpose. Your author, for one, has spent many hours staring into the void of Outlook and Teams chats, questioning his very existence – and he has gathered plenty of other anecdotal evidence of colleagues harbouring similar feelings of dejection during his career in public relations (PR).*

Finally, the rise of jargon can also be attributed to its *practicality*.

In the bullshit jobs ecosystem, rarely is anything definitive. Black or white. Right or wrong.

If we look at the work of a farm labourer, there is a correct time to sow a certain crop, based on the season, on the local climate and on years of know-how. There is also a correct time to start the day (sunrise) and to end it (sunset).

But for a PR professional, there is no objectively right time to issue a press release or to kick off a campaign about a new product. There's not even an obviously right time to begin and conclude your working day anymore, especially with remote working and a globalised economy. There are just different shades of right.

As a result, language that avoids definitive statements is exceedingly helpful. It allows us, for instance, to test the water without committing to anything that might

---

* As an aside, PR and its sibling professions marketing and advertising account for a large proportion of jobs in the 'services industry', identified by Graeber as a growth area for bullshit employment. Sometimes termed 'the creative sectors', these disciplines – and the firms and people working within them – have provided the most fertile ground of all for the creation and harvesting of jargon.

backfire later. Why promise to deliver something by 5 p.m. when you can say 'end of play' instead?

Buzzwords also give us the practical tools we need to navigate one of the toughest workplace occurrences of all: conflict.

It's no coincidence that the rise of jargon coincided with the decline of aggressive or overly authoritative behaviour at work. The stern or shouty CEO, once respected, is now out of fashion. To raise one's voice in a meeting is more likely to be the death knell of your career than to recommend you to the board. Yet, disagreements and the need to correct shoddy work still exist in the same volume as they did before.

Jargon allows us to deliver critiques without coming across as too malicious. 'This work isn't good enough' has become 'Let's find a way to up-level this idea'. Although, in turn, this has ushered in the arguably worse era of passive-aggression.

So, fuelled by a desire for *authority* or an urge to *belong*, by a thirst for *self-worth* as well as the need for *practical* tools to survive the modern workplace, we have collectively initiated an avalanche of linguistic bullshit. And this is a phenomenon that has so much momentum that it cannot now be stopped.

Instead of succumbing to this deluge and being metaphorically suffocated beneath the sheer mass of terminology, your only option is to slalom through working life with a firm grasp of what constitutes a 'tiger team', with an ability to differentiate your 'townhalls' from your 'all hands', and with an understanding of when it is appropriate to create a 'war room'.

Circle Back: The Little Book of Business Buzzwords was written to help you navigate the confusing world of corporate speak and to ease you down a gentle downslope to linguistic cognisance.

Enjoy.

CIRCLE BACK!

A

A business receives 'air cover' from the PR team.

✦ above the line/below the line

A categorization of marketing and advertising tactics. 'Above': highly visible but untargeted (such as a TV ad or a billboard poster). 'Below': work aimed at specific people (like a direct mail campaign). 'Through the line' has emerged as a phrase to describe work that arguably ticks both boxes – posts on social media, say. These terms are regularly used inaccurately.

✦ across the detail

An indication one has a grip on the situation or knows the ins and outs of what is happening. The question of whether a person is across the detail is only ever asked by someone senior addressing a subordinate – or uttered in reverse to reassure a manager you have got a handle on things (usually because you do not).

COO:	Were you aware of the environmental backlash to Slug Energy's 'Just Use Oil' campaign?
Harriet:	… I'm across the detail …

✦ actions

Items of work that need doing. They form one's to-do list, particularly for juniors.

◆ air cover

Positive publicity to distract an audience from stuff you have done wrong.

Harriet: Give me an update on 'Just Use Oil'.
Will: Well, Facebook mentions have topped a million, James O'Brien has set up a pressure group on his LBC radio show, and people have started coating the head office windows in oil …
Harriet: We need air cover. Resend that press release about us sponsoring a Namibian ballet school.

◆ align/alignment

The process of making sure that everyone who needs to be aware of a decision or piece of work is up to speed. Ensures one is not left solely to blame should anything backfire.

MD: How the hell did 'Just Use Oil' even get signed off?!
Harriet: Well, we aligned with you and your leadership team last quarter, during the **all-hands** meeting …
MD: Ah.

◆ all-hands
A meeting or call that everyone is expected to attend. Usually involves a whole department or organization. Almost always dull and missable.

◆ always-on
A piece of work that runs indefinitely with no set end date, e.g. daily tweets from a corporate account.

◆ annual leave
Time off work. For unknown reasons, the word 'holiday' should be avoided professionally. Other accepted alternatives include PTO (paid time off) and OOO (out of office), neither of which should ever be spelled out in full.

◆ asset(s)
A flexible term covering all things that comprise a piece of work or help deliver it. These usually include digital documents, such as press releases, folders of images or video content.

Chad:	Sally, I've been checking out your assets. Let's just say I like what I see …
Sally:	Umm, do I need to call HR?
Chad:	What? No! The Monster Crunch crisp campaign assets! The Insta posts are spot on!

B

A creative director with a lot of 'balls in the air'.

◆ baked-in

When something is included or embedded in something else.

Client:	I think the plan is great, but it doesn't have anything about advancing our sustainability goals?
Elizabeth:	Oh, green proof-points will be baked-in to all the **hero thought leadership** content. That way your **messaging** cut-through will be market-leading!
Client:	In English, please, Elizabeth …

◆ balls in the air

A creative way of saying you are busy. Can be used to ward off an incoming **action**. Less extreme than **snowed under**.

Chad:	Have either of you got time to proofread this press release?
Sally:	Sorry, I've got a lot of balls in the air at the moment …
Jimmy:	I'm totally snowed under mate …
Chad:	It'll have to be you then Sal. Within the hour please!
Sally:	(FFS!)

♦ bandwidth

Another way of communicating how busy somebody is. More likely to be used by management when ascertaining who has the capacity to take on a task.

Elizabeth:	We've got a new business pitch coming up next week. Chad, can you or someone in the team help do some desktop research regarding the media landscape?
Chad:	Sure – I believe Sally has bandwidth.
Sally:	(FFS!)

♦ best in breed

The best possible version of something. A term often used by agencies to differentiate their idea from that of a rival firm, despite it being largely identical.

Client:	And how will you ensure our CEO gets in front of the top consumer lifestyle correspondents?
Elizabeth:	With Peddle PR's best-in-breed media relations programme!

♦ big bets

The decisions or pieces of work you really want to be a roaring success. Often means more resources or budget will be made available. Usually uttered discreetly, so as not to overinflate expectations in case of failure.

◆ big rock(s)

Your main priorities. But, just to keep you guessing, this term might be occasionally used as a way of describing your challenges, i.e. a rock being an obstacle.

Sally:	[Stressing] I feel there's too much on the team's plate at the moment. There's no way we'll get through all this by the end of the week!
Chad:	[Assuredly] Focus on the big rocks.
Sally:	(WTF?!?)

◆ blue ocean

An area/subject/idea that has not yet been explored. Grander in scale than **whitespace**.

Jimmy:	Well, in terms of topics, we think AI is the whitespace for us …
Chad:	Goddammit man! We're beyond whitespace here – where's the blue ocean?!
Elizabeth:	[Nods approvingly]

◆ blue sky

Relates to approaching or thinking about something in a positive, novel or creative way. One should avoid 'grey sky thinking' at all times.

◆ blue thread

Something – such as a topic or **message** – that connects multiple pieces of work or plans. Why it is usually blue remains a mystery – 'white thread' is sometimes also used with the same meaning.

◆ boiling the ocean

To overcomplicate something or increase a project's scope to the point it becomes doomed to failure.

Jimmy:	Then, we'll attach a giant Monster crisp packet to a hot air balloon and fly it over London.
Chad:	By giant, we mean frickin' enormous …
Jimmy:	The balloon will be piloted by GMTV's Mr Motivator, who'll be singing that song by The Automatic on a loudspeaker.
Chad:	WHAT'S THAT COMING OVER THE HILL? IS IT A MONSTER?! IS IT A MONSTERRRRRRR!
Elizabeth:	… I feel like we're boiling the ocean with this one.

◆ boilerplate

A paragraph – found at the bottom of a press release – that describes what a company does. Less a piece of jargon and more an accepted (but very weird) idiom that no one will ever explain to a new starter. Derived from the phrase 'boilerplate text', which covers all forms of precreated content that can be copied and pasted whenever needed, with no changes to the original needed. The term emerged in the early newspaper industry, where metal printing plates used for typesetting of prepared content were likened to the rolled steel elements of a hot water boiler.

◆ brain dump

To write down/discuss all things relating to a particular topic. Often seen as the start of a creative process. Used by management to get juniors to type up their great ideas.

Sally:	I don't even know where to begin with the revised Monster Crunch campaign. It's stressing me out!
Chad:	Maybe you need a dump?
Sally:	Sorry?!
Chad:	A brain dump. Let's get the **tiger team** together and get our **ducks in a row**.

◆ brainstorm

A meeting with the specific purpose of generating new ideas. This is so well established in common parlance that it only just merits inclusion here. Survived a period of disapproval after suggestions of political incorrectness.

◆ brand

An organization, product or person with a distinct/curated identity. The word 'brand' is used flexibly in creative sector workplaces: as a noun, a verb and/or an adjective. For example, a marketing agency might describe clients they work for as 'brands' and/or they might use 'brand/branding' to describe their own services.

Interviewer:	So, what would you say your greatest strength is?
Chad:	[Muses for a while] ... Brand **storytelling**.
Interviewer:	... Ok. And your biggest weakness?
Chad:	If anything, I'm too passionate about telling stories for brands.

◆ brickwall

An opportunity that is hard to tackle but offers significant results/rewards if achieved.

◆ bringing back the dodo

Trying to resurrect a nice but critically flawed idea.

Jimmy:	Perhaps Mr Motivator could be driving a monster truck instead?
Elizabeth:	Jimmy. No one under 50 knows who Mr Motivator is ...
Chad:	Yeah, you're trying to bring back the dodo with this one, bud.

♦ burning the clutch

When someone tries to make a change, or **pivot** a project, in a clumsy manner.

♦ business impact

The perpetual conundrum creative professionals face: how does one demonstrate to one's client or boss that one's work has any tangible effect? (Spoiler: it often does not.)

Client:	What was the business impact of the campaign?
Jimmy:	Well, the press release received five pieces of media coverage, including prestigious publications such as *Data Centre Dynamics*.
Client:	We sell printers.
Jimmy:	[Sighs]

♦ buy-in

Getting other people (often the budget holders) to back your idea. Using the term implies their support is in doubt.

Chad:	So, we're going to drop a giant crisp packet in the Thames then let it float down to Tower Bridge. Guaranteed coverage in the daily papers, and sh*t tonnes of Insta posts.
Elizabeth:	Love it. What are the next steps?
Chad:	Buy-in from the client. We're **opening the kimono** in the meeting tomorrow.

C

Account directors 'circling the wagons'.

◆ caviar to kale

When something (or someone) threatens to transform a piece of work from a classy-looking proposition to something altogether more unappealing.

Harriet:	The CEO loves your **roundtable** idea – great work. However, he wants to change the venue.
Will:	But the World Trade Centre is the perfect setting for an oil commodities conference?
Harriet:	He feels Mar-A-Lago will better suit the delegates the board have in mind …

◆ chameleonize

When an idea or piece of content can be adapted for a new purpose.

Jimmy:	FFS, Elizabeth wants us to have a deck ready for the Pepsi new business pitch by EOW!
Sally:	How are we supposed to get that done in two and a half days?!
Chad:	Chillax gang. We pitched for the Coke account last year – just chamleonize the deck.
Sally:	As in …
Chad:	Ctrl + F. Change all 'Pepsi' mentions to 'Coke'. Oh, and the logo on the front. Simples.

Jimmy: ... This explains why we never win any new business.

◆ change agent

A bringer of change. Can be applied flexibly, such as in relation to an idea or individual (often with questionable levels of sincerity).

Jimmy: I mean, what does Elizabeth even do, other than being a classic account dictator?*
Sally: I dunno – Chad said she's been a real change agent throughout her career.
Jimmy: [Pretends to be sick]

◆ change gears

To stop doing or talking about one thing and begin something else instead. Can be used passive aggressively to imply your topic/action is more important (i.e. a higher gear).

◆ circle back

To return with updates or recommendations. Usually uttered by middle managers to juniors to ensure nothing is being overlooked.

---

* Introducing a new term: 'account dictator', meaning an account director/leader who has a fondness for discipline.

◆ circle the wagons

Gathering together a group of people from different parts of the business. Done to either pool knowledge/resources or to stop disparate teams working on the same thing.

Will:	I've just heard sales are already working on a 'sustainability summit'. Shall I set up a meeting?
Harriet:	I'd rather you circled the wagons.

◆ come to Jesus

A moment of sudden realization that leads to major change. Usually deployed to convey how another person or group will be brought (somewhat forcibly) round to a certain point of view. Can also express the need for an individual to improve their personal performance.

Elizabeth:	I feel like Jonny is slacking.
Chad:	I think you mean Jimmy.
Elizabeth:	Whatever. The new one.
Chad:	He's been here three years.
Elizabeth:	I think it's time for a lil' come to Jesus conversation ...

◆ core competencies

Stuff you should be good at. Only ever uttered by someone pointing out where you need to improve.

Jimmy: I've been an account executive for almost three years. Have I not done enough for a promotion?

Elizabeth: Jonny, I'm afraid Chad thinks your core competencies need further development. And I agree.

D

A junior account executive takes notes
during a 'deep dive' session.

◆ deck
Document used for a presentation. Always PowerPoint slides. The term 'slide deck' goes back to an era where slides were physically inserted into a projector and beamed onto a wall or screen. These slides could be manually reordered. Doing so was likened to shuffling a deck of cards.

◆ deep dive
To go into something in more detail. Alternatively, use **double click**.

◆ deliverables
Stuff you are on the hook to do. Used more often in agencies/consultancies, where there is an external client for whom the work is being 'delivered'.

◆ dial down
Do less of something. Usually a precursor to abandoning an idea entirely.

Head of Sales: [Mischievously] Hey, is your 'Just Use Oil' campaign still running?
Harriet: We've decided to dial it down.

◆ dial-up
Do more of something. Often accompanies a dialling down so as not to appear like less work is going on overall.

Head of Sales:	[Mischievously] Quiet time for the marketing team then?
Harriet:	[Snorts] We've actually dialled-up our emerging-markets cultural arts campaign.
Head of Sales:	Namibian ballet?
Harriet:	[Nods]

♦ double click

To go into something in more detail. Alternatively, use **deep dive**.

Sally:	Well, that's the final slide currently. How long did that take me to talk through?
Chad:	About 20 minutes.
Sally:	Hmm, we'll probably have time in the meeting to cover something else …
Chad:	Let's double click on the **blue sky** thinking audit.
Sally:	Double what?!

♦ drill down

Like **double click**, this means to go into something in more detail but more from an exploratory point of view. That is, to uncover something new.

Client:	I appreciate the **blue sky double click**. But we could really do with a deep dive

	on the topics raised – especially how sewage firms are leveraging AI.
Chad:	We'll drill down on sewage and come back to you next week.
Client:	Sounds lovely.

◆ drink the Kool-Aid

To follow or do something without question. In a business environment this term is used to suggest that a person or team needs to get on board with an idea and just accept the direction of travel, regardless of any (likely legitimate) concerns. The term has rather grisly origins, relating to the mass suicide of a cult in the late 1970s, where members drank a substance similar in appearance to the US flavoured drinks brand Kool-Aid (no doubt presenting the company with a permanent publicity headache).

Jimmy:	I really feel we should rethink the marital aid campaign. Floating something large down the Thames is so 2012!
Chad:	Five words Jimbo. Drink. The. Kool. Aid … … … Now.

◆ driving up the mountain pass in fifth

To lose momentum rapidly (like a car going uphill in fifth gear).

♦ ducks in a row

To get organized (for once). Usually uttered if senior management sense things are not on track. Often results in a fraught meeting, disguised as a **huddle**, or creation of a **tiger team**.

E

The brand marketing team at 'end of play'.

◆ elevate

A flexible term, most commonly used to express a need for improvement (but without explicitly telling someone their initial effort was dire). Can also instruct someone to send work up the chain of command for review, ensuring plenty of scope for confusion.

Elizabeth:	Jonny, can you elevate those AI sewage bylines?
Jimmy:	Sure! Who do they need to go to? Straight to the client?
Elizabeth:	No, elevate them. They currently read like crap.
Jimmy:	Excuse the pun!
Elizabeth:	What?
Jimmy:	Doesn't matter.

◆ end of play (EOP)

The end of the working day. Usually uttered in relation to a deadline. An exact time is almost always left undefined, and often interpreted very differently by the deadline giver and receiver.

Harriet:	I asked you to get that social asset timeline sent across by end of play Tuesday.
Will:	Uh huh – did you not see my email?
Harriet:	I assume you mean the mail at 11.59 p.m.
Will:	That's the one.

◆ evangelist

The creator or representative of a new idea or way of doing things. Usually a self-appointed title.

> Kind regards,
> Harriet Stern
> Marketing Evangelist
> Slug Energy

◆ evergreen

Something that will be of use for a long period of time. Could be a campaign idea or a specific **asset** like a blog.

F

A remote employee enjoys another 'fireside chat'.

◆ fireside chat

Deployed to give a corporate conversation a (false) sense of intimacy and honesty or a feeling that it is relaxed. Almost certainly will not take place next to a fire and nor will it ensure that someone resists speaking predominantly in jargon.

Head of HR: Employee morale has hit an all time low. Any chance of raising salaries to keep up with inflation?

CEO: [Chortling] Let's just do another fireside chat about macro headwinds. That'll get us through another year.

◆ flight time
The length of time that a piece of work or project will take to complete.

◆ flywheel
An idea or campaign that will intrinsically gather momentum (such as through public interest and noise on social media) and continue delivering positive results. Very rarely, if ever, achieved.

Elizabeth:	So, all the sculptures will be made from actual Monster Crunch crisps?
Chad:	Yep. And by hosting the exhibition in Trafalgar Square, we'll get tourists sharing images on their socials all summer, further boosting reach internationally!
Elizabeth:	This has got all the makings of a flywheel campaign. Nice work.

G

Ad agency exec demonstrating a 'growth mindset'.

◆ go to market

In sales, this means to start selling a product or service. Used in the creative sectors as a way of saying you are going to activate a piece of work.

Harriet: I love this idea. Good job team. Let's go to market.
Yasmin: Oh, the street food vendors only come on Thursdays. Pret's open though?

◆ growling at the grizzly

Openly disagreeing with, or pushing back against, a ferocious superior – thus entering into a battle you cannot win.

Yasmin: Have you seen Harriet's email? She's telling me to '**elevate**' the slide deck for an eighth time! I'm going to **push back**.
Will: I wouldn't. You'll just be growling at the grizzly.

◆ growth mindset

Harder to grasp than smoke. Usually a very ambiguous way of describing (or asking for) willingness and ambition. A useful tool for senior management to encourage junior employee zeal or improved performance but without committing to specifics that might lead to notions of a promotion or pay rise.

Jimmy: [Exasperated] I've hit all the goals we set last year and demonstrated my **core competencies** consistently. What else do I need to do to make account manager?!

Elizabeth: Ever heard of a little thing called growth mindset?

H

The sales team conduct a 'huddle' before the big pitch.

◆ hard stop

A way of saying you need to end a conversation at a specific time because you have another engagement. Usually leveraged to get out of a meeting, regardless of whether you actually have something after it.

Jimmy:	Good meeting – I'll circulate **actions**. Oh Chad, it'd be great to have a quick chat about my development. Apparently, I need a **growth mindset** to …
Chad:	[Heading towards door] Sorry mate, did I not mention I had a hard stop at half past? Gotta dash!

◆ hero

Applied to whatever **asset** or 'thing' in your plan is the best. Used to describe whatever the top piece of content you have created is (e.g. the best video of a new product).

◆ hit(s)

Alternative term for a piece of media coverage. Encompasses everything: from a news piece in a national broadsheet to an article on a news aggregator site no one will ever read. Useful for reaching targets without any indication of quality. Can also refer to webpage link clicks.

Chad:	So, gang – how many hits has the Monster Crunch campaign got so far?
Sally:	[Checks notes] Err, three if you include that student paper with seven readers.
Chad:	We need more **hits**! Everyone on the phones. I've said it a million times, this client is all about the hits!
Jimmy:	[Under breath] I'd like to hit you.
Chad:	Huh?
Jimmy:	Nothing mate.

♦ hive mind

A prefix to asking a group of colleagues a question, almost always via a messaging app or email. Often used by senior management to appear informal, to distract from their own deficiencies, or to disguise the fact they are delegating a task.

Yasmin:	Has Harriet even started the PR strategy presentation? It's due to the CMO by EOP.
Will:	[Looking across office] I can see her screen from here – looks like she's still on the title slide. Oh wait, she's typing on Teams …
Harriet:	[Via 'Comms Dream Team' group chat] 'Hive mind! Has anyone seen any clever brand campaigns recently? If you could pop them on a slide, that'd be fab x'

◆ huddle

A form of meeting. Use of a cosy-sounding word implies the get-together will be more informal and open than a regular meeting. This is rarely the case as huddles are most often deployed by managers in times of crisis or stress.

I, K

The new corporate comms strategy is 'in the fog'.

♦ ideation
The process of coming up with creative ideas. A term that has also begun making its way into dreadful job titles.

> Kind regards,
> Harriet Stern
> Head of Marketing and Ideation
> Slug Energy
> Cannes Award Winner 1992

♦ in the fog
Describes a project or team that has gone off course.

♦ influencers
Umbrella term for anyone who could conceivably make customers think differently or buy something. Often the worst people in society.

♦ insights-driven
The use of data or facts to make a decision, rather than your usual approach of simply guessing at what might work.

> **Sally:** This survey says '62% of consumers are fed up with brands doing brash stunts, like plonking giant products in London'.
> **Jimmy:** But, this one says 83% of TV watchers miss Mr Motivator ... So, we're up on aggregate!

◆ integrated
A piece of work where multiple disciplines/tactics are utilized or in which more than one team/department is involved. Often promised, rarely realized.

◆ KPIs
Key performance indicators, i.e. results you are on the hook to deliver.

L

B2B content strategist making sure their idea 'ladders up' to the firm's objectives.

♦ ladder-up
When a piece of work connects with or complements a bigger project.

♦ lean in
Multiple meanings. Most commonly used to describe getting closer to something, such as a particular subject matter, piece of work, team or individual. Alternatively, committing to an activity or plan more fully.

Yasmin:	David from the social media team is running a campaign about the best items of furniture to burn for heat this winter. Should we **align**?
Harriet:	Let's lean in first.
Yasmin:	(???)

♦ lighthouse
A lighthouse customer is an early adopter of a company's products/technology. A lighthouse project is something that is small in scale but promises to show the way to something bigger. Lighthouse leadership is the act of guiding your team through a particular issue. A lighthouse moment is an instance of success or recognition. Ample room for confusion.

◆ long tail

Activity or results that will be delivered over a longer period of time. Often uttered to allay fears an initial launch has flopped.

Elizabeth: [Looking disapprovingly at a PowerPoint deck] So, for the launch of our client's latest brand of rubber gloves, your campaign generated a single piece of coverage in *Kitchens Quarterly*?

Chad: A tier-one hit. And don't forget, the long tail is only just beginning to swing!

Elizabeth: Meaning …?

Chad: A byline in *The Cleaner's Chronicle* …

◆ low-hanging fruit

Easy work with guaranteed (but expected/unspectacular) results.

Sally: I've tried everywhere. No one is interested in writing about rubber gloves, even if they do have [reads press release] 'aerodynamic properties'!

Chad: Time to pick the low-hanging fruit. Tell *Cleaner's Chronicle* we'll give them 500 words on how cleaning gloves are leveraging F1 technology.

M

The thought leadership tiger team
attempt to 'move the needle'.

◆ messaging
The things you want to say about a particular subject. Can be in relation to a specific product or a whole organization – and everything in between. Used by firms as a guide for all written and verbal communications, to ensure control and consistency.

◆ mission critical
A crucial item of work that cannot be messed up. Rarely turns out to be that important.

◆ mission statement
A way for a company to articulate what they do without saying 'we sell stuff', or for a team to articulate their reason for existing. Can also be termed 'vision' (although **narrative** bores will insist on differentiating the two).

◆ moments in time
Fixed dates or events that shape a piece of work or a campaign.

◆ moonshot
An ambitious project or idea, normally included in a pitch by an agency attempting to show off its creative capabilities to a client. The vast majority of these concepts fail to gain sign off.

Chad: I think we need to add a moonshot element to the Monster crisp deck before the client meeting.

Jimmy: Are you telling me Mr Motivator in a hot air balloon didn't qualify as a moonshot?!

♦ move the needle

To make a significant difference, usually on a large scale, i.e. to change opinions across a whole industry or to radically improve performance.

Elizabeth: [Finishing presentation with a flourish] And with this **integrated** communications programme, we'll leverage U-BND's suite of products to really move the needle on the debate around hygiene in the post-pandemic era!

Prospective client: You do know we just sell toilet brushes?

N

Employees following the CEO's 'north star' goal.

♦ narrative
Another way of describing what it is you would like to say. Confusingly, it can be used interchangeably with **messaging**. However, narrative often differs in the sense it covers a wider scope – acting as an umbrella term under which can be found multiple messages.

♦ nerve centre
A room or other defined area in which a team meets to work on a specific project. Similar to a **war room** but usually used for longer-running bodies of work.

Elizabeth:	Why isn't Susan in the **war room** working on our new client podcast offering? You know this should be her top priority.
Chad:	Err, I think you mean Sally? She's actually in the social media nerve centre, two meeting rooms along.

♦ net new
Something that is actually new – not a recycled idea or rehashed content (which represents 90% of work in the creative sectors).

♦ newsflow
The chronological order of things you are going to announce/publicize.

◆ north star

A figurative reference point to guide everything you do. Usually leveraged by very senior people to try and give some semblance of purpose, gravitas or grandeur.

CEO:	This is why our north star going forwards is INTEGRITY. The integrity our founders showed all those years ago will shape every action this firm takes.
Journalist:	Including the new cobalt mine you opened yesterday in war-torn Ethiopia?

◆ NPI

New product introduction. An acronym that has never once been spelled out.

Harriet:	[Via email] BTW, JB is OOO next week so he can't present the B2B NPI slides in the AGM. WDYT about the CTO discussing the ROI of the new B2C CMS instead? Internal comms want our POV by EOP. Oh, and the PMO's RACI slide will need updating too.
Yasmin:	Apologies, can you clarify next steps?
Harriet:	[Automatic reply: I am OOO on PTO for the rest of the week. Please contact Yasmin Newt for all queries.]
Yasmin:	(FML)

◆ nudge

A repeated attempt to elicit a response, such as a reply to your last eight emails. Can imply use of informal channels of communication, like Teams chat or WhatsApp.

Sally:	Hey, just nudging you again about last week's press release. Do you think the RubbaTron 3000s might make your next issue?
Journalist:	Strangely, condom launches aren't a focus area for the *Financial Times* right now. Please delete my number.

◆ nuggets

Units of information or points of interest.

O

An ambitious sales lead considers 'opening the kimono'.

♦ OGSM
Objectives, goals, strategies, measures. Normally used in planning documents/slides.

♦ on the bleeding edge
When a piece of work is truly groundbreaking or close to being controversial. Rare.

♦ onboard
Bringing a new person into the team. Also allows the use of 'offboard', which sounds a whole lot better than demoted or sacked.

♦ one throat to choke
When a single person or team is responsible for a piece of work or a campaign, thus making them easier to hold to account. Usage frowned upon by HR.

♦ open the kimono
Reveal your idea or a new level of detail. Nothing to do with exposing yourself. Usage panics HR.

Harriet:	In our next one-to-one, I'm going to open the kimono …
Will:	(Please don't.)
Harriet:	… on next year's **NPI roadmap**!
Will:	(Phew.)

- **organic**

Used in PR circles to describe results, such as media coverage, that were achieved without paying for them. Can be used more broadly to signify a serendipitous occurrence.

P

The head of innovation decides to 'pivot' the campaign. Again.

♦ pain point
Something preventing progress.

Chad:	Jimmy, mate, the team are telling me you're struggling. What are your pain points?
Jimmy:	I've been an account exec for four years and still flat share with eight people in Clapham.

♦ paradigm shift
A wholesale change. Usually because whatever you were doing before was not working. More sudden than **moving the needle**.

♦ pencil in
Temporarily agree to something, normally before backing out – like a meeting you cannot be bothered with.

Elizabeth:	Look, you're not far off account manager!
Jimmy:	Great. Well, I'm overdue a formal appraisal. Can we arrange one?
Elizabeth:	Sure, let's pencil that in for next Friday …

♦ pick your brain
A gross way of asking for someone's opinion. Can precede a **brain dump**.

♦ pillar(s)
The defined elements of a project, plan, **narrative**, etc.

♦ ping
To message someone, likely using a form of communication other than email. Similar, but more informal than a **nudge**.

♦ pivot
To completely change direction with a piece of work. Similar to, but less dramatic than, a **paradigm shift**. Not to be confused with the popular Excel function.

♦ playbook
A compendium of all the work (strategies, plans, tactics, etc.) a team plans on doing, usually over the course of a year. Sometimes called a 'bible'.

♦ PMO
Project management office. Akin to a tiger team but less cool and more permanent.

♦ POV
Point of view. An opinion. Rarely personal or genuine, but one that fits the **messaging/narrative** of one's organization.

♦ push back
To resist doing something for someone, without simply saying no (as that would be deemed far too aggressive for the modern workplace).

♦ push the envelope
Going beyond normal expectations. Often used to glamorize an idea.

CEO:	So, how are we going to claw back all the credibility we lost with 'Just Use Oil'?
Harriet:	Well – we've really pushed the envelope with this idea. Will – **open the kimono** …
Will:	[Reading slide with dread] Introducing our new campaign: 'Coal is Cool', fronted by brand ambassador, and former Premier League star, Carlton Cole.
CEO:	Seriously? He's not even the most famous Cole in football!
Harriet:	Ashley, Joe and Andy weren't short of cash …

♦ put a pin in it
To stop working on something. Either to declare it finished or, more often, because one wants to consign a bad idea to the scrapheap.

Will:	… 'Coal Goals' will also serve as a **north star** for the whole business …
CEO:	Put a pin in it.

R

A journalist after another PR intern attempts to 'reach out'.

♦ RACI

Responsible, accountable, consulted, informed. A system used to designate how integral people are to a project or campaign. Often seen in overly bureaucratic planning processes.

♦ reach out

To get in touch with someone, usually for the first time, and often by way of an unsolicited email or LinkedIn message.

> Hey,
> Hope all is well.
> Off the back of the recent RubbaTron 3000 launch, I just wanted to reach out to see if you would be interested in an 800-word byline about next-generation prophylactics?
> Kind regards,
> Sally
> Senior Intern, Peddle PR

♦ red flags

Potential issues to be aware of. Usually given to a spokesperson ahead of a media interview so they are prepared for tricky questions.

♦ rip the plaster off
An unattractive way of saying 'let's stop hesitating and get on with it'. Usually needed with an idea no one is keen on.

♦ rising tide
Shortened from the phrase 'a rising tide lifts all boats'. It means that better macro conditions will benefit all.

♦ roadmap
A plan of action, often with **moments in time** included.

♦ rolling thunder
Building momentum over an extended period of time, rather than relying on one big moment. Usually used around a product/service/event launch.

Elizabeth: Take me through the rolling thunder approach. This has to go off with a bang!

Chad: [Energized] OK, first we tease some images on the corporate Twitter account. Then we drop a few cryptic clues via the CIO's LinkedIn page. Then we've got an exclusive interview with *Infrastructure Ideas Magazine* on the morning of the Data Centre Dynamics trade show, where the ServatudeZ7 will be on display!!

Elizabeth:	Sorry, what are we launching again?
Jimmy:	[Despondently] A cooling system for IT servers …

♦ roundtable

A meeting where an (often boring) topic is discussed by multiple experts. Rarely happens at a round table. A conversation between two speakers should be termed a fireside chat instead.

♦ run it up the flagpole

To check the popularity or viability of something, such as a creative campaign idea.

S

An agency's new social media guru applies their 'secret sauce' to the project.

◆ sandbox
A safe or controlled space in which to test more adventurous ideas/concepts.

Sally:	Is there such a thing as a bad **brainstorm** idea?
Chad:	Are you in a sandbox?
Sally:	Metaphorically? Yes.
Chad:	Then, no!

◆ secret sauce
Your competitive edge. Applied when selling-in a project or idea.

Jimmy:	I'm nervous about this new business pitch.
Chad:	Don't worry, it's in the bag. I've spread my secret sauce all over it.
Jimmy:	… Gross.

◆ segue
Declaring a desire to move from one topic of conversation to another, usually during a fraught meeting.

◆ share of voice
How much publicity a company is getting in comparison to its rivals. Used by PR professionals when analysing press coverage. Figures are usually massaged favourably.

♦ ship it
Uttered when something is finished and good enough for submission/sending on.

♦ silos
Teams working in isolation, to their detriment. Nothing to do with grain or farms.

♦ sizzle reel
A compendium of your best work, often in a multimedia format (such as a video compilation).

♦ snackable
Something short and easily digested. Often used in relation to a piece of content, such as a tweet or blog.

♦ snag list
All the issues hindering a project. Can also describe outstanding **actions**. The term originated in the construction sector as a list of small faults in a building, but it is beginning to migrate to the creative sectors.

♦ snowed under
Busy and/or overwhelmed with work. Often uttered to ward off an incoming **action** regardless of whether you have capacity or not, or simply to sound the part in front of management. Trumps **balls in the air**.

MD:	How are things Harriet?
Harriet:	[Aloud] Totally snowed under at the moment. You know how it is!
Will:	[Aside, under breath] She took yesterday's Zoom call from a Bannatyne Spa. I could see the logo …
Yasmin:	Ah, I thought that looked like a dressing gown.

♦ socialize

To share a plan or document between teams, usually within your own organization. Similar to **alignment** but more relaxed, usually implying the work or idea is in its formative stages.

♦ splash deck

A series of slides that show off your greatest work. Similar to a **sizzle reel** but PowerPoint orientated.

Chad:	That splash deck looks great Sally. Let's **run it up the flagpole** with Elizabeth then **ship it** to the client.
Sally:	Oh great, so we're speaking in semi-nautical jargon now?
Chad:	Huh? By the way I'm cruising to The Anchor for a tankard after work if you fancy it?

◆ stakeholder(s)

Used internally, this means the people you are beholden to for a piece of work – a list normally headed by whoever is funding the project. Externally, the term refers to your audiences. Either way, if you do not know who the stakeholders are, you are likely doing it wrong!

◆ stand-up

Another fancy name for a meeting to make it seem less boring. Can imply it is a meeting where spoken updates are given by all attendees (normally while sitting, staring at a Zoom screen).

Sally:	Ah, Chad's in the waiting room, I'll let him in.
Elizabeth:	Chad, you're late for our stand-up. Again.
Chad:	Apologies gang. You see, it overlaps with the digital team's **townhall**.
Elizabeth:	Why are you attending that? I told you to prioritize the consumer org's **huddle**.
Chad:	Ah, they've shifted that back an hour, clashing with corporate comm's weekly **touch base**.

◆ storytelling

A more glamorous (and nauseating) way of describing the art of communicating. This is often used in PR and marketing circles and increasingly found in awful job titles.

> Kind regards,
> Harriet Stern
> Marketing Evangelist, Head of Ideation and
> Brand Storytelling
> Slug Energy

◆ stretch assignment
A new task in addition to your day-to-day responsibilities. Usually a menial job someone more senior does not fancy doing, given under the pretence it will prove your suitability for promotion.

Chad:	Hey Jimmy! Jimbo! The J-man. [Slaps back] I've got a stretch assignment for you. It'll be great experience!
Jimmy:	Sure, I'm game!
Chad:	Can you collect the sandwiches from Pret and lay out the meeting room?
Jimmy:	[Sighs]

◆ sweat the assets
To ring every last drop out of something: maximizing use of a piece of content, for example. Could conceivably also be applied to junior team members.

Client:	If we do go with your campaign idea, how will we ensure return on investment?
Elizabeth:	By sweating the assets!
Client:	... Should we run that past legal?

♦ swim lanes

Topics for an individual or organization to focus on, thus becoming a **thought leader** on the matter. Similar to **whitespace** but more detailed.

Elizabeth:	[Waves dismissive hand] I can't do your appraisal then. It clashes with the CEO's swim lane call.
Jimmy:	Oh ... ok. I'll push it another week then?
Elizabeth:	Remind me – what swim lanes did we identify at the **whitespace** meeting?
Jimmy:	[Checks notes] Erm, a blog series on investing in your staff ...

♦ sync

To talk to someone. Can be used as another term for a meeting.

♦ synergy

Where different ideas, pieces of work, or even whole teams complement each other.

T

**The product marketing team consider
their next 'tentpole' moment.**

◆ take offline

An instruction to set up a separate chat to cover a topic that has arisen during a meeting or conversation. Almost always conducted online still.

Jimmy: I just feel we can't keep coming up with ideas that involve floating something down the Thames. Clients aren't going for it!
Chad: Let's take this offline.
Jimmy: Sure, I'm in the office tomorrow?
Chad: Let's do a Zoom on Friday.

◆ talent

Either prospective employees or a way to describe celebrities/**influencers** you intend to work with.

◆ tentpole

The central or stand-out moment in a campaign. The term has been imported from the film industry, where a tentpole movie would bring in enough money to compensate for less successful offerings.

◆ territory

An area of ownership within a wider piece of work.

◆ thought leadership

Famously overused term to describe an organization displaying an opinion, usually through content attributed to a senior leader. Rarely are these opinions noteworthy due to bureaucratic sign-off processes whittling away anything interesting.

◆ thought shower
Replacement term for **brainstorm**, in case the latter causes offence.

◆ thunder and lightning
Specific moments within a long-running campaign that aim to grab customer attention. Akin to a flurry of **tentpoles**.

◆ three-sixty (360)
All encompassing. Similar to **wholistic**. Often used around appraisals, i.e. feedback has been sought from a wide range of sources.

◆ tiger team
A group put together to address a specific problem, usually by someone that does not want to do the job themselves. Often an unglamorous task, hence the use of 'tiger' to add an element of otherwise-absent excitement.

MD: Team morale seems low. Can we get some ideas for a decent Christmas do?
Chief of Staff: I'll have Sandra in HR form a tiger team.

◆ tissue session/meeting

The presentation of an idea/plan under a guise of informality. Usually arranged by an agency when there is a fear their ideas are rubbish and will otherwise be torn apart by the client.

Jimmy:	This is the third straight year our **hero** idea has been based around creating a giant packet of Monster Crunch … I'm just not sure how it'll go down in the client presentation?
Chad:	Fear not Jimbo, it's just a tissue meet!

◆ top of the mast head

The starting moment or the most visible element of a campaign, such as a press release announcing the launch of a new product.

◆ touch base

Another form of meeting, but more likely a one-to-one catch-up with a colleague or professional acquaintance. Never used outside of work despite the term's ubiquity. Almost certainly originated in the United States from baseball parlance.

◆ townhall

Yet another type of meeting. Often deployed for large-scale affairs instead of **all hands** to foster a sense of community and team spirit (usually indicating something bad is being announced).

◆ tracking
A way of confirming that you are listening/understanding.

Client:	If I see one more slide with a giant packet of Monster Crunch on it, you're fired.
Chad:	Tracking.

◆ turn the lights on
Reveal detail or get something started. No negative connotations, unlike **ripping the plaster off**, and less likely to spark panic than **opening the kimono**.

◆ turnkey
Something that is complete and ready to use straight away. Borrowed by PR types from the tech industry, where any product that solves a problem immediately is sold as a 'turnkey solution'.

U,V

Toothpaste ad team opt for another totally genuine customer 'voxpop'.

◆ under the UV
Putting something through a more thorough examination, revealing flaws others might have missed.

Jimmy:	I want to be in the pub by 5 p.m. I'll just use Chat GPT to write this LinkedIn blog.
Sally:	Don't! Elizabeth's putting all client **thought leadership** content under the UV.

◆ up-level
To make something better. Allows a reviewer of a piece of work to request improvements without using terms that are increasingly frowned upon in the modern workplace – such as 'rubbish' or 'crap'. Similar to **elevate**.

◆ vox pops
Short interviews, normally done informally to camera with members of the public or users of whatever you are trying to sell. The phrase comes from Latin, meaning 'voice of the people'.

W

An account executive 'wordsmithing' a press release after the seventh round of client feedback …

◆ war room
When a team gathers in a specific place to work on a task, such as calling journalists about a new product launch. If a **tiger team** convenes in an area with four walls, there is every chance it becomes a war room.

◆ wheelhouse
Things you are good at or responsible for, or that fall within your sphere of influence – from items of work, to skills, to people.

Chad:	How come you weren't on the 3 p.m. call?
Sally:	Oh, I had to attend Google Ad training.
Chad:	Neat – you can add that to your wheelhouse!

◆ white glove
Indicates something is of high quality. Usually to do with events but can be applied to more mundane work such as content creation.

◆ whitespace
An area/subject/idea that has not already been done to death by someone else. Not dissimilar to **swim lanes**, but broader. Identifying it is often the start of a new **thought leadership** programme.

Sally:	We've got to create five LinkedIn blogs for the CEO of this logistics firm by the end of the month.
Chad:	Yikes.
Sally:	What on earth are we going to write about that people will actually click on and read?
Chad:	[Muses] Have you tried identifying the white space?
Sally:	(???)

◆ wholistic

Alternative spelling of 'holistic'. Both are used liberally across the creative sectors to imply work is all encompassing or involves multiple disciplines.

◆ wordsmithing

Literally, editing words to make something sound or read better. Used when only minor improvements are needed, unlike **up-level** where a more major overhaul is required.

◆ workback

A written account of everything that needs doing to complete a big piece of work. Essentially, a compendium of **actions** and **deliverables**. Workbacks are time-consuming and usually needless admin (handed almost exclusively to junior team members).

Jimmy: [Handing over gift] Sal, I got given you in secret Santa. Merry Christmas!
Sally: [Unwrapping] Wow: *The Little Book of Business Buzzwords*! Thanks Jimmy.
Chad: [Observing] Useful – should give you a real three-sixty account of the corp lingo we use round here.
Sally: Three-what?
Jimmy: Page 94 …

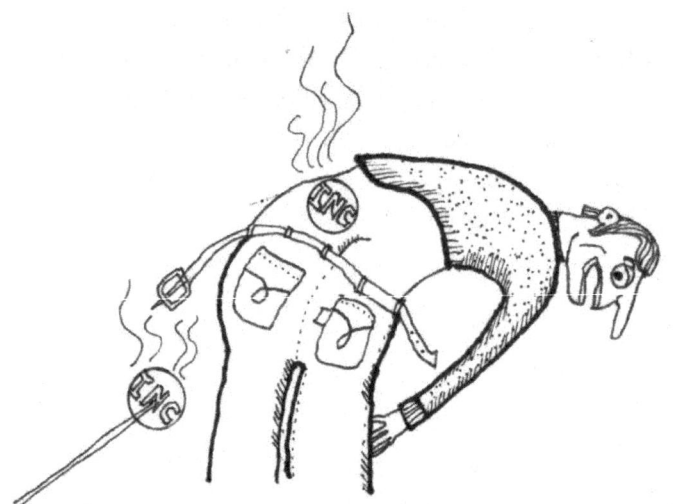

'CORPORATE BRANDING'

About the author

George Baggaley is a communications and marketing professional based near London, England. His early career saw him working for a number of the city's top PR agencies before later moving in-house at a major American tech firm.

This range of experience has given him a front-row seat to the linguistic pantomime performed each working day in the creative industries. Across many years of brain dumps, huddles, ideation sessions and townhalls, he made a habit of jotting down buzzwords in the margins of notebooks as and when they were uttered. It is those scribbles that have been collated to form this book.

X/Twitter: @GeorgeBloggaley
Bluesky: @georgebaggaley.bsky.social

Thank you!

Circle Back! The Little Book of Business Buzzwords has been independently compiled and marketed by me, the author, after a decade of navigating the jargon-infested world of corporate communications. Thank you so much for buying it!

If you've enjoyed the book, I would be eternally grateful if you tweeted/posted about it with a link to the publisher's website (see QR code below) or wrote a review on Amazon or on the book's Goodreads page.

If there are any buzzwords you feel should be included but aren't, feel free to **touch base** on email or **reach out** on Instagram and I'll **circle back** with a second edition!

Email: circle.back@hotmail.com
Instagram: @business_buzzwords